JE SCHU

Schuett

I am caring /

P9-EDW-367

I Am
Caring

by Sarah L. Schuette

Consulting Editor: Gail Saunders-Smith, Ph.D.

Consultant: Madonna Murphy, Ph.D.
Professor of Education,
University of St. Francis, Joliet, Illinois
Author, *Character Education in America's
Blue Ribbon Schools*

Pebble Books

an imprint of Capstone Press
Mankato, Minnesota

Pebble Books are published by Capstone Press
151 Good Counsel Drive, P.O. Box 669, Mankato, Minnesota 56002
http://www.capstone-press.com

1 2 3 4 5 6 07 06 05 04 03 02

Library of Congress Cataloging-in-Publication Data
Schuette, Sarah L., 1976–
    I am caring / by Sarah L. Schuette.
    p. cm.—(Character values)
    Summary: Simple text and photographs show different ways of being
helpful and showing that you care.
    ISBN 0-7368-1438-8 (hardcover)
    1. Caring—Juvenile literature. [1. Caring.] I. Title. II. Series.
BJ1475 .S34 2003
177'.7—dc21   2001007796

Note to Parents and Teachers

The Character Values series supports national social studies
standards for units on individual development and identity. This
book describes the character value of caring and illustrates ways
students can care about themselves and others. The images support
early readers in understanding the text. The repetition of words
and phrases helps early readers learn new words. This book also
introduces early readers to subject-specific vocabulary words, which
are defined in the Words to Know section. Early readers may need
assistance to read some words and to use the Table of Contents,
Words to Know, Read More, Internet Sites, and Index/Word List
sections of the book.

Table of Contents

THANK YOU FOR YOUR DONATIONS

E SORRY, BUT WE CANNOT
PT THE FOLLOWING ITEMS:

Torn or Dirty Clothing
Broken Electrical Items
Chemicals or Paints
Large Appliances
Dehumidifiers
Air Conditioners
Tires

4

I am a caring person.
I think about the needs
of other people.

I care about my family.
I give my dad a hug. I
tell him that I love him.

I listen to my sister when she is sad. I try to help her feel better.

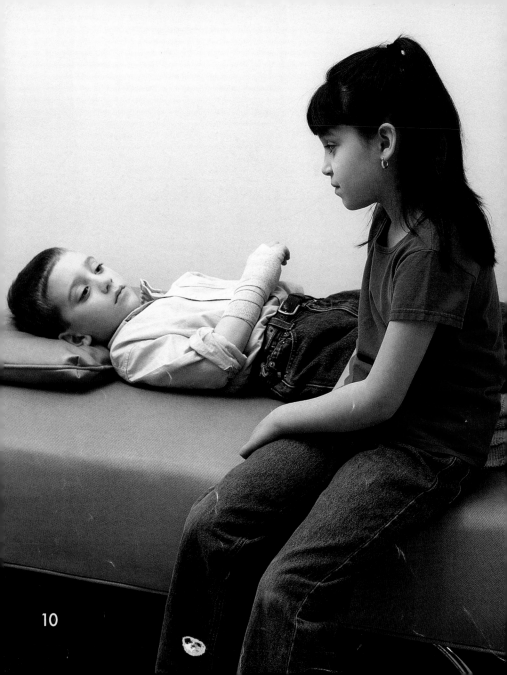

I care about my friends.
I visit my friend
when he is hurt.

I tell my friend that
she did a good job.

I care about animals.
I take care of my pets.

I care about my safety.
I wear my seat belt
in the car.

I care about my health.
I eat good food.

20

I am caring, thoughtful, and kind. I think about myself and others.

Words to Know

caring—being concerned about a person or a thing; caring people pay attention to other people's feelings.

kind—to be friendly, helpful, and generous

listen—to pay attention so that you can hear something; caring people pay attention and listen to others.

sad—an unhappy emotion; caring people listen and support others who are sad.

thoughtful—to consider other people's needs and feelings; thoughtful people think carefully before they make a decision; they sometimes put other people's feelings before their own.

visit—to go to see a person or a place; caring people visit other people when they are sick or hurt.

Read More

Lewis, Barbara. *Being Your Best: Character Building for Kids 7–10.* Minneapolis: Free Spirit, 2000.

Maurer, Tracy. *A to Z of Helping Hands.* A to Z. Vero Beach, Fla.: Rourke, 2001.

Raatma, Lucia. *Caring.* Character Education. Mankato, Minn.: Bridgestone Books, 2000.

Internet Sites

Adventures from the Book of Virtues
http://pbskids.org/adventures

Amazing Kids
http://amazing-kids.org

Kids Can Make a Difference
http://www.kids.maine.org/cando.htm

Kids Care Club
http://www.kidscare.org

Index/Word List

Word Count: 114
Early-Intervention Level: 9

Editorial Credits

Mari C. Schuh, editor; Jennifer Schonborn, series designer and illustrator; Nancy White, photo stylist

Photo Credits

Capstone Press/Gregg Andersen, cover, 10, 12; Gary Sundermeyer, 1, 4, 6, 8, 14, 16, 18, 20

Pebble Books thanks the Moreno family of Mankato, Minnesota, for modeling in this book. The author dedicates this book to her aunts, Lois and Ruth Schuldt, of Belle Plaine, Minnesota.